WHO LIVES UNDERGROUND?

A SONG ABOUT WHERE ANIMALS LIVE

By TOM DAVID BARNA

Illustrated by TIM PALIN

Music Arranged and Produced by MARK OBLINGER

CANTATA LEARNING

WWW.CANTATALEARNING.COM

CANTATA LEARNING

Published by Cantata Learning
1710 Roe Crest Drive
North Mankato, MN 56003
www.cantatalearning.com

A note to educators and librarians from the publisher: Cantata Learning has provided the following data to assist in book processing and suggested use of Cantata Learning product.

Publisher's Cataloging-in-Publication Data
Prepared by Librarian Consultant: Ann-Marie Begnaud
Library of Congress Control Number: 2015958171
Who Lives Underground? : A Song about Where Animals Live
Series: Animal World : Animals at Home
By Tom David Barna
Illustrated by Tim Palin
Summary: An interactive song about different creatures that live underground.
ISBN: 978-1-63290-604-5 (library binding/CD)
ISBN: 978-1-63290-659-5 (paperback/CD)
Suggested Dewey and Subject Headings:
Dewey: E 591.5648
LCSH Subject Headings: Animals – Habitations – Juvenile literature. | Animal ecology – Juvenile literature. | Underground ecology – Juvenile literature. | Animals – Habitations – Songs and music – Texts. | Animal ecology – Songs and music – Texts. | Underground ecology – Songs and music – Texts. | Animals – Habitations – Juvenile sound recordings. | Animal ecology – Juvenile sound recordings. | Underground ecology – Juvenile sound recordings.
Sears Subject Headings: Animals – Habitations. | Animal behavior. | School songbooks. | Children's songs. | Folk music.
BISAC Subject Headings: JUVENILE NONFICTION / Science & Nature / Environmental Science & Ecosystems. | JUVENILE NONFICTION / Music / Songbooks. | JUVENILE NONFICTION / Animals / General.

Book design and art direction, Tim Palin Creative
Editorial direction, Flat Sole Studio
Music direction, Elizabeth Draper
Music arranged and produced by Mark Oblinger

Printed in the United States of America in North Mankato, Minnesota.
072016 0335CGF16

ACCESS THE MUSIC!

SCAN CODE WITH MOBILE APP

CANTATALEARNING.COM

Did you know that many animals live underground? They dig tunnels through dirt and rock to make their homes. These animals live in homes called dens, nests, **burrows**, and **warrens**. Living underground helps animals stay safe.

Turn the page to find out who lives underground. Remember to sing along!

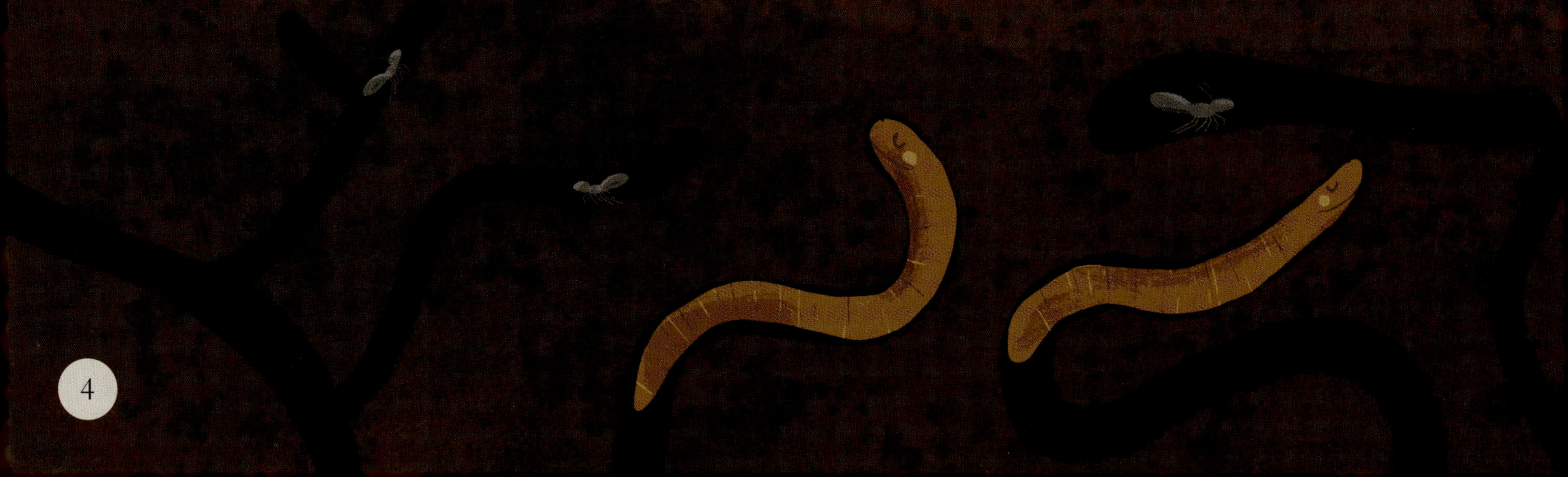

Who lives underground,
hopping up and down?

Is it a moose
hopping all around?

A jackrabbit lives underground,
living in a bunny town.

Rabbits live underground.

Who lives underground,
marching up and down?

Is it a rhinoceros
marching all around?

There are **harvester** ants underground,
living in an ant town.
Rabbits and ants live underground.

Who lives underground,
squirming up and down?

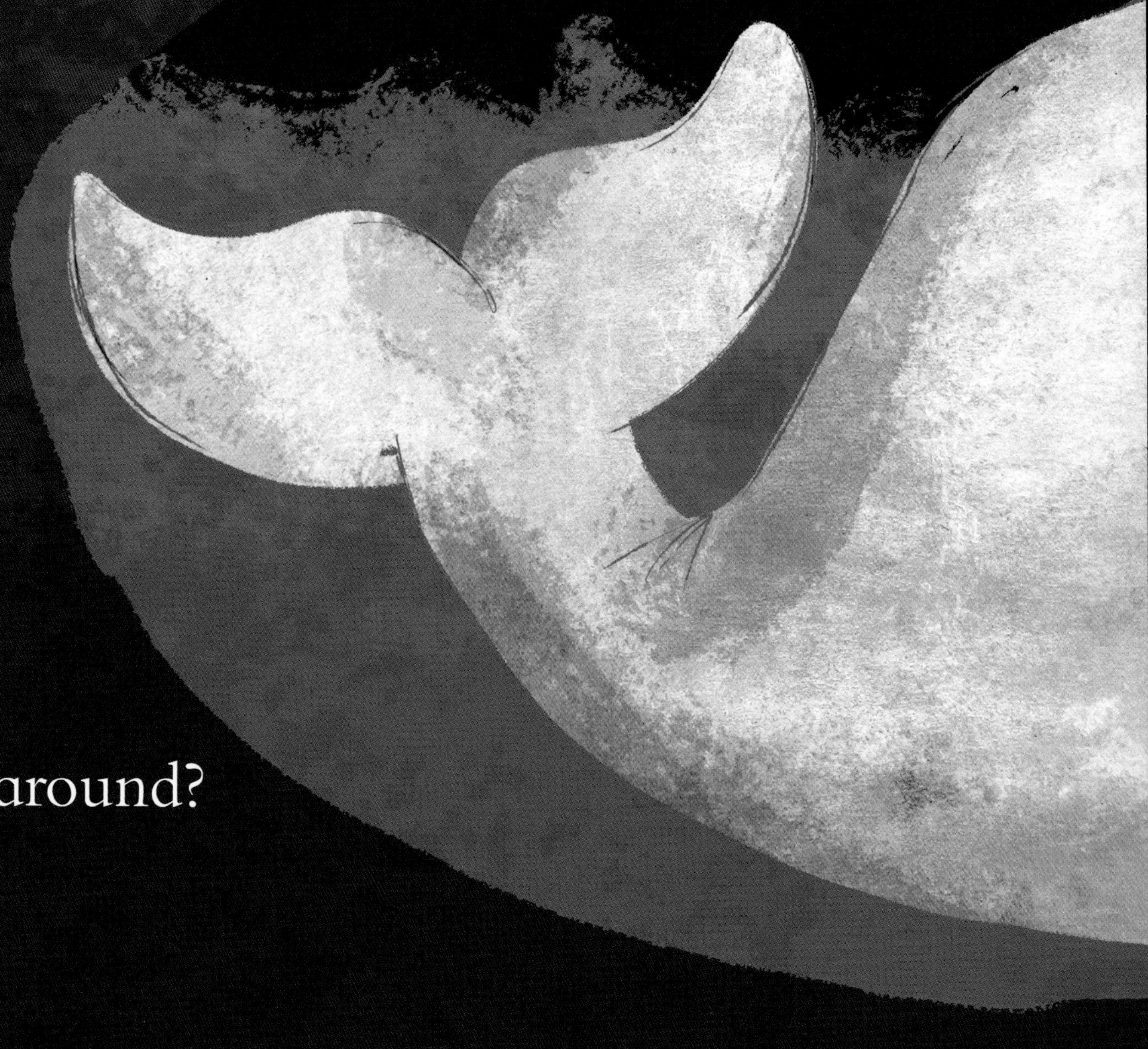

Is it a whale
squirming all around?

No!

An earthworm lives underground,
living in a worm town.

Rabbits, ants, and worms live underground.

Who lives underground,
crawling up and down?

Is it a horse
crawling all around?

A star-nosed mole lives underground,
living in a mole town.

Rabbits, ants, and worms,
and moles live underground.

SONG LYRICS

Who Lives Underground?

Who lives underground,
hopping up and down?
Is it a moose
hopping all around?

No!

A jackrabbit lives underground,
living in a bunny town.
Rabbits live underground.

Who lives underground,
marching up and down?
Is it a rhinoceros
marching all around?

No!

There are harvester ants underground,
living in an ant town.
Rabbits and ants live underground.

Who lives underground,
squirming up and down?
Is it a whale
squirming all around?

No!

An earthworm lives underground,
living in a worm town.
Rabbits, ants, and worms live underground.

Who lives underground,
crawling up and down?
Is it a horse
crawling all around?

No!

A star-nosed mole lives underground,
living in a mole town.
Rabbits, ants, and worms,
and moles live underground.

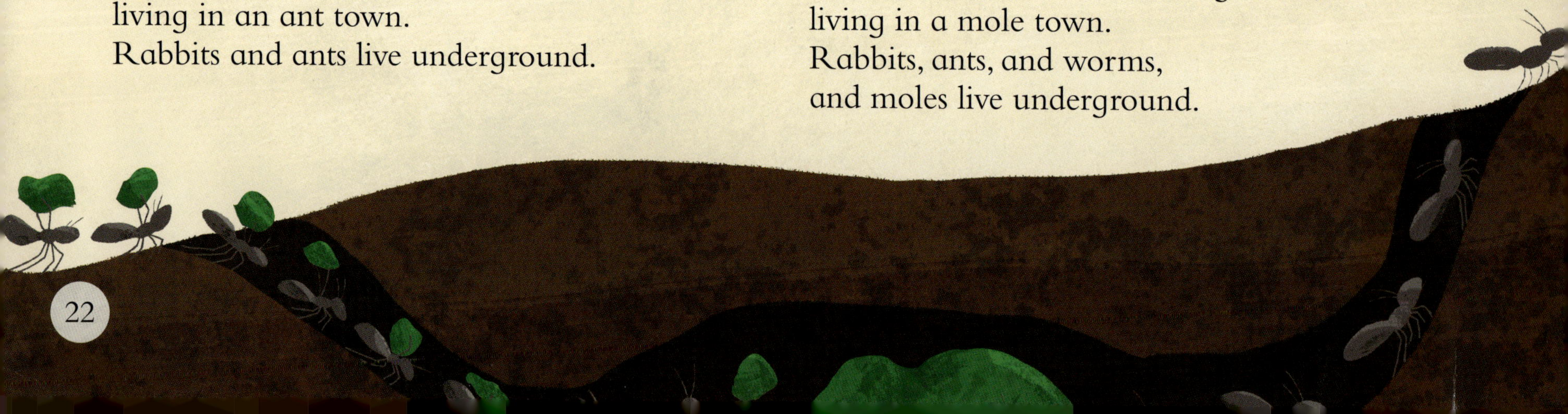

Who Lives Underground?

Americana (Pop)
Mark Oblinger

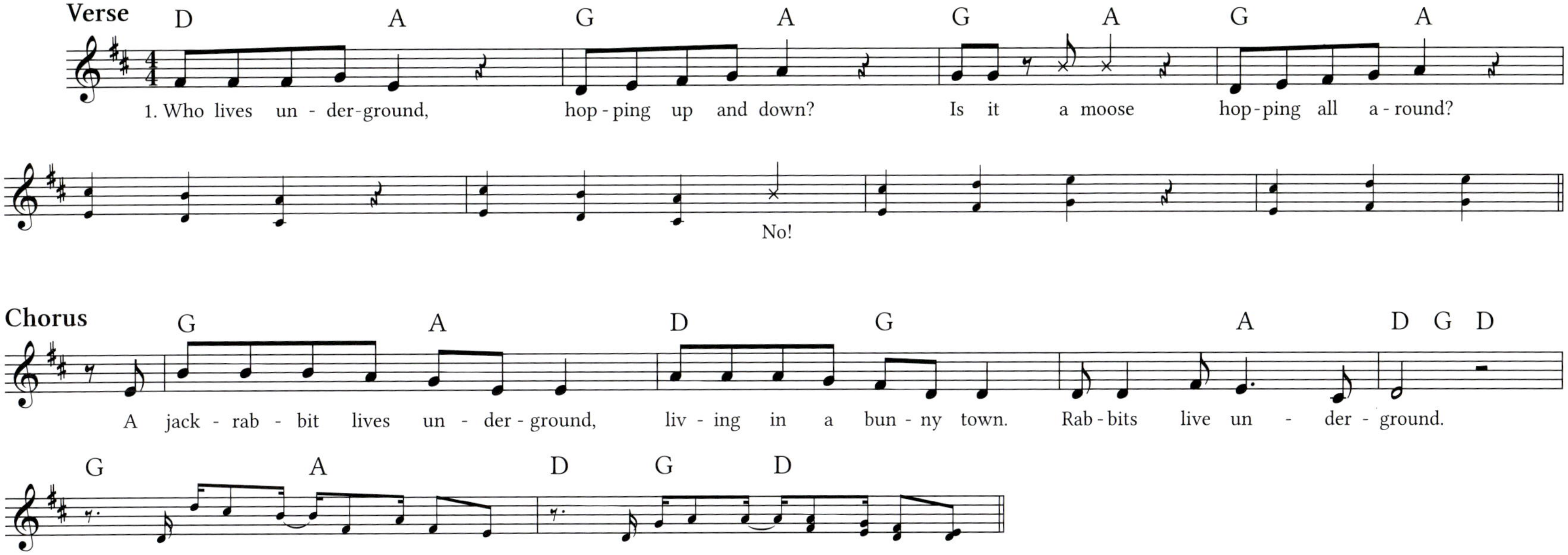

Verse 2
Who lives underground,
marching up and down?
Is it a rhinoceros
marching all around?

No!

Chorus
There are harvester ants underground,
living in an ant town.
Rabbits and ants live underground.

Verse 3
Who lives underground,
squirming up and down?
Is it a whale
squirming all around?

No!

Chorus
An earthworm lives underground,
living in a worm town.
Rabbits, ants, and worms live underground.

Verse 4
Who lives underground,
crawling up and down?
Is it a horse
crawling all around?

No!

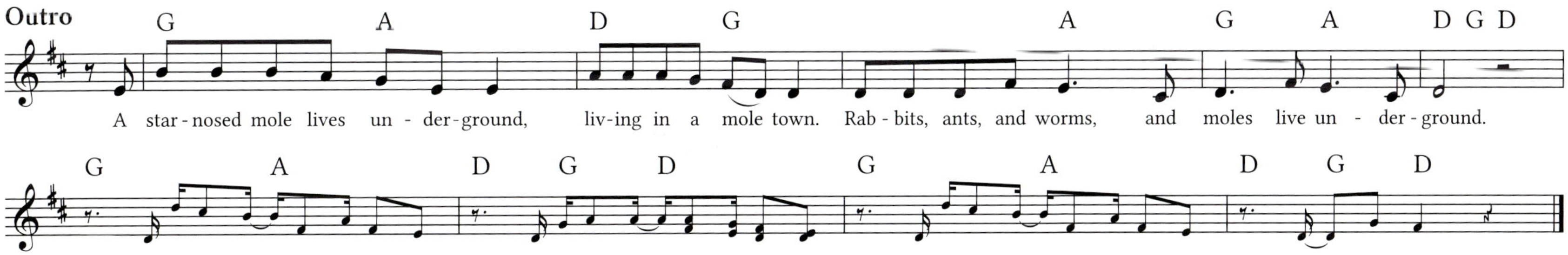

GLOSSARY

burrows—holes or tunnels in the ground that animals make to live in

harvester—a person or animal that gathers food

squirming—twisting or moving

warrens—series of underground tunnels where rabbits live

GUIDED READING ACTIVITIES

1. Rabbits, ants, worms, and moles live underground. What other animals might live underground?

2. Do you see rabbits, ants, or worms above ground? When do you see them? Why do you think they sometimes come above ground?

3. What do you think it would be like to live underground? Draw a picture of your underground home.

TO LEARN MORE

Clapper, Nikki Bruno. *Earthworms*. Mankato, MN: Capstone Press, 2016.

Rake, Jody Sullivan. *Meerkats, Moles, and Voles: Animals of the Underground*. Mankato, MN: Capstone Press, 2016.

Rustad, Martha E. H. *What's in the Dirt?* Mankato, MN: Capstone Press, 2016.

Schuh, Mari. *Rabbits.* Mankato, MN: Capstone Press, 2015.